How Much Can You Save?

There are five options to consider as the general contractor who is building their own house. With this book, I will show you how to save 10-to-21%. The more you do, the more you save.

OPTIONS	POTENTIAL SAVINGS
1. General Contractor I 　　a). Hire a Foreman at 0.28-.035% of total cost. 　　b). Sub-Contract each phase.	10% - 12%
2. General Contractor II 　　a). Sub-Contract each phase.	12% - 15%
3 General Contractor III 　　a). Sub-Contract major work. 　　b). Sweat Equity (see Checklist in Appendix).	15% - 17%
4. General Contractor IV 　　a). Sub-Contract HVAC, Electrical & Plumbing Only. 　　b). Hire Crews for remainder.	17% - 19%
5. General Contractor V 　　a). Sub-Contract HVAC, Electrical & Plumbing Only. 　　b). Sweat Equity (see Checklist in Appendix). 　　c). Hire Crews for some jobs.	19% - 21%

Things to Consider...

One of the biggest reasons to act as your own general contractor is the money you can save by investing your time and energy, also known as 'Sweat Equity,' into your home-building experience. Another consideration that you need to keep in mind is the mental and emotional involvement, also known as 'Intellectual Effort,' in building your own home.

Whether you are having your home built for you, or you decide to act as your own general contractor, you need to keep in mind that both avenues have some stress involved because this is **your home** that is being built. While you may have heard some horror stories from people who have undertaken such a project, you will also feel a great sense of satisfaction, pride and fulfillment when your home is complete.

How can I make that claim you ask? Simple. I have 40+ years of building experience. The key to acting as your own general contractor with the least amount of stress possible is being aware of the steps and procedures. This will make the process more enjoyable and it will save you 10's of thousands of dollars.

To help you with this, I have created this guide covering such topics as land purchase, living options while you are building, construction and permanent financing loans and most important of all, I will show you how and where you can save money!

Additional Services Offered: I have also included a section on additional services that I can provide to assist you, the owner/general contractor, during your building process.

Disclaimer: The designer of this program has put substantial care and thought into this guide. However, because we may not be providing direct supervision of the program's use, as well as unknown environmental conditions such as soil, seismic, weather conditions, including great variances in local building practice, we cannot make any warrant, expressed or implied, with respect to the content or use of this guide.

The owner/purchaser shall take full responsibility for the implementation of this program. This guide is designed to provide accurate and authoritative information regarding the subject matter. It I sold with the understanding that the author and publisher are not engaged in rendering legal, accounting or other professional services. If legal advice is required, the service of a competent professional should be sought.

Terms and Conditions: This program is protected under the terms of the United States Copyright Laws and may not be reproduced or copied in any way, by any means, unless you have written permission from the author. It is for the explicit use of the purchaser only.

Table of Contents

CHAPTER 1

How Much Can You Save?	3
First Things First	5
On to Your Dream Home	5
Financial Viability	6
Temporary Housing & Storage Needs	6
Additional Services	7
Additional Information	7

CHAPTER 2

Down to the Nuts & Bolts – Start Up	8
Land	8
House Plans	9
Building Materials	11
Materials Bid	12
Paperwork, Insurance, Other Services	13

CHAPTER 3

Financing	14
Scheduling & Construction	14
Additional Thoughts	15

CHAPTER 4

Building Advisory Group Services	16
Notes	18

APPENDIX

Minimum Square Footage Checklist	20
Desired Rooms Checklist	21
Home Style Checklist	22
Sweat Equity Checklist	23
Taxes Checklist	24
Additonal Considerations Checklists	25
Building Advisory Group Contact Information	26

© 2012 BUILDING ADVISORY GROUP

CHAPTER 1

First Things First – The Three W's

The first thing you need to think about and decide is **"Why – Where – When"** do you want to build your own home.

Why? Instead of a cookie-cutter home, by building your own place you get to choose all of the important features, such floor plan, interior and exterior finishes and room layout – this is especially important in the kitchen, laundry and living room areas. An added benefit is that you have the satisfaction of investing something of yourself into the home when you design and help build it. AND… you can save money by acting as your own general contractor!

Where? Do you want to live in the city limits or in the country? Are there lots in the city limits that you are partial to? Is there a certain area of the county you are interested in, and are there lots/acreage available? I'll cover more on this topic further along in the guide since there are several items to consider.

When? If you plan on acting as your own general contractor, you might want to consider any vacation time you have available to take during the building process so you can be "on-site" during the day. When you are deciding on this part of the equation, keep in mind that there are several steps that need to be completed prior to actually starting the work. I will go in detail later in the guide.

On To Your Dream Home

The next thing you want to think about is the style of your dream home. I have included a "House-Style Checklist" in the Appendix that covers such items as square footage, roof type and materials, siding and elevation.

Also in the Appendix of this guide, I have included a checklist for the desired rooms, the recommended square-footage of the rooms, as well as any out-crop buildings you may want to include on your property. You can add or subtract any additional rooms or square-footag.

These checklists in the Appendix are designed to help you get a general idea of the style and size of the home you want to build. This information will also assist you when looking at building sites and house plans.

On Your Financial Viability

The next thing you want to consider is your financial viability. How much capital (savings/investment) do you have that can be applied towards building your dream home?

How much sweat equity are you able and willing to invest into this process? For this, you will need to have the knowledge, tools and time to complete each section of the building that you want to complete yourself. For example, you can save money by painting the inside of the home with a few simple tools and time. However, painting the exterior of the home requires different tools – such as sprayers and a different level of expertise. So the important thing about sweat equity is to <u>be realistic</u> in you evaluation of the projects you can and can't do yourself. Please see the "Sweat Equity Checklist" in the Appendix.

Next up is to talk with banks or lending institutions that do construction loans and see how much money you can qualify to borrow (pre-qualify) for an interim construction loan, as well as for permanent home financing. This crucial information will help guide your final decisions on location, home style and amenities.

Temporary Housing

An important point to consider during the building process is to address your housing needs and what to do with your furniture/possessions. I won't be covering this area in depth, but will list some options that you can consider.

Housing Needs:

1) Rent back – if you sold your primary residence, you may want to consider asking the buyer about renting back the house until your new home is complete.

2) Rent house or apartment.

3) Rent motel/hotel.

4) Rent space or live with relatives.

5) RV or trailer that you can live in at a park or move on your property. If you own an RV and there is room on your new property, you may want to consider living on-site during the construction process. Not only will you be at the work-site, you will be able to save money on rent.

Furniture & Possessions

As I mentioned previously, you will need to do something with your personal possessions. Here are some suggestions:

1) Sell – this is a good time to go through your furniture and possessions and sell items you no longer want or need to own. It can also save you money on storage fees by having less to store.

2) Donate – if you are willing, this is a "feel-good" option for thinning out your things. This can also save you money on storage fees by having less to store.

3) Storage Rental (Local Unit or On-Site) – if you have the room at the building site, you may want to consider renting a portable storage unit. This will allow easy access to your possessions and once the home is complete, you will be able to move items quicker and easier into your new home. This will also save you money on gas and any truck rentals required to move your items.

Additional Services

Now that we have looked at important considerations you should have before becoming your own general contractor, I want to again remind you that you don't have to do it alone. As an owner of this guide, Building Advisory Group (BAG) has an additional range of services that can assist you during any phase of your construction project. These services are outlined in Chapter 4.

Additional Information

Throughout the remainder of this guide, I will continue to expand upon subjects already discussed, along with money-saving ideas and tips. And although your local area may require additional paperwork, I will go over the basic paperwork you will need to complete during your home project. Be sure to check with your local building department, planning and zoning and/or your chamber of commerce. And again, the Checklists in the Appendix are designed to assist you with your decision-making.

CHAPTER 2

Down to the Nuts & Bolts – Start-Up

LAND

    Whether you are planning on purchasing land/lot for building, now or in the future, there are several things you need to consider. Some of these options apply if you are going to build now, while others only apply if you are planning on building later.

A) Purchasing Considerations from:

  1) Individuals – do they have clear title?
  2) Developer – front footage, easements and appreciation
  3) Realtor – corner lot, right-of-way and dimensions
  4) Website – grade, flood zone and open lot

B) Location Considerations:

  1) Restrictive Covenants
  2) Cost of Property
  3) Home Owner's Tax
  4) Proximity to Work
  5) Proximity to Schools and Parks
  6) Proximity to Shopping, Hospitals and Health Care
  7) Proximity to Emergency Services – Ambulance, Fire & Police Departments
  8) Flood Zones
  9) Surface Water
  10) Contaminate Noise (i.e. Airplanes)
  11) Traffic – now and in the future
  12) Zoning in Adjacent Areas – S1, S2, S3, C-1, C-2?
  13) Right of Ways and Easements
  14) Special Purpose Areas
  15) Bike and Hiking Paths
  16) Water Purification & Sewage Treatments
  17) Airports
  18) Landfills
  19) Utilities – Electric, Gas, Propane, Water, Sewage, Septic, Telephone & Cable
  20) Land Preparation – Clearing

It is always a good idea to check with your local planning and zoning department about any future plans for the surrounding areas. You may have found the perfect area and then find out they are planning on putting in a highway by-pass next to your property – talk about noise and the potential decrease in property value in the future.

Remember – you are not just looking at the land and the surrounding areas in its current state, you need to plan for what it will look like in the future too!

HOUSE PLANS

Now that you have an idea as to the type of house you want to build; talked with the lending institutions about your financial viability; and found the land/lot you want to build on, it is time to find some home plans that fit your needs. There are several places you may want to consider:

1) Local Builder/Designer.
2) Magazine/Book/Website.
3) Architect.
4) Plan with Basement, Wood Floor or Slab on Grade.
5) Does Plan come with Materials List?
6) Cost of Addendums, Changes or Alterations.

Once you have your plans in hand, it is extremely important to scrutinize the plans carefully. In most cases, any changes you make to the plans are going to cost additional money. Here are some of the items you need to be looking at while going over your plans, as well as some areas that can save you money. Checklists in the Appendix will assist you with this as well.

I) Exterior
1. Foundation – many need to alter this to meet local codes.
2. Number of Corners – inside/outside – roofline. All corners add to cost.
3. Height of Walls – you may want to have a 10-12 foot or higher ceilings but remember the higher the wall, the more sheet rock and insulation that is required. This adds to your cost, along with additional heating and cooling costs.
4. Ceiling Framing.
5. Size of Rooms.
6. Pitch and Style of Roof and Overhangs.
7. Window & Skylight Size & Type – check for energy efficient windows and skylights. Over the long run, you will save money in energy costs and may qualify for government energy rebates.
8. Exterior Walls & Insulation.

9. Exterior Door Size & Type – check with local, state and federal agencies for energy rebates.
10. Type of Exterior Finish.
11. Cut-in or Truss Roof
12. Roof Materials – shingles, tile, metal or other. NOTE: when choosing your roofing material, consider metal roofing as it may qualify for energy rebates.
13. Hose Bibs & Sprinkler Systems
14. Fence – retaining walls, gates, driveways, sidewalks & planter boxes.
15. Fireplace.
16. Overhead Doors.
17. Size of Water Meter.
18. Out-Crop Buildings – barns, sheds, etc.
19. Passive or Active Solar – water, wind, fuel type (natural gas, oil, LP, electric, etc.).

II) Interior
1. Height and placement of walls, arches, columns, pass-thru, amount of openings and doors, right angles, etc.
2. Floor – wood, concrete, flat, stepped, angle, bump outs, offsets, etc. (consider renewable resource flooring, if possible).
3. Sound Abatement
4. Plumbing Layout and Fixtures
5. Cabinets and Counter Tops – layout, style & price range
6. Electrical Plan and Light Fixtures
7. Total Electric, Electric & Gas, etc.
8. Appliances – check for energy efficient appliances with Rebates
9. Built-in Storage and Closets
10. HVAC Size & Type
11. Finish Flooring
12. Wall Finish – texture, paint, wallpaper, etc.
13. Interior Trim – style, size, paint, stain, etc.
14. Doors – locksets, cabinet hardware
15. Bathroom – mirrors, shower doors, etc.

Once you have your final house plans, you need to make sure it fits the land/lot you have decided to purchase. Some additional items to consider at this point are:

1) Presentation and Alignment of the house on the property – exposure.
2) Trees and other vegetation currently on the land – will you need to remove it or can you design around it. The more you remove, the higher the cost.

3) Utility Access to Property – this includes electric, gas, water, sewage, cable and telephone. Will you need underground or overhead utilities for electric, cable and telephone service? Having utility poles put in can cost you extra. The same goes for water, sewage and gas. The longer the span to tie into the service, the more it will cost you.
4) Landscape Placement – type of restrictions may increase/restrict water use.
5) Driveway Needs
6) Don't Over Build. By this I mean, if the area you plan on building has current development, check with your local real estate agency to find out the market value of the surrounding homes. If the neighborhood homes have a market value less than your dream house, you may not be able to regain equity. Again, check for any restrictive covenants.

Building Materials

If you purchased your home plans from a local builder, you may want to talk with them about supplying the materials list for the project to see if you can save some money.

If you purchased your home plans with a materials list, you can now break them down so you can present them to suppliers for bids.

However, if you don't have a materials list with the plans, you will need to put one together. You can consult with a local builder or local building supplier for assistance with this part of the project.

You will also need to make sure that when you are putting together your materials list that you break it down by line item/category. For example:

1) Materials
2) Labor
3) Taxes
4) Sub-Contractors
5) Clean-up Cost – If you choose to do this yourself as sweat equity, you will need to rent large dumpsters and pay for disposal costs. Check with local companies in your area for prices.

MATERIALS BIDS

You should have three bid packages that include all taxes, insurance and license requirements that breaks down as follows:

1) Material + Tax + Labor
2) Labor + Tax
3) Labor Only – includes all men and tools necessary
4) Material Types Specified – size, grade, etc.
5) Pay Self for Sweat Equity – labor and administration, including office, supplies, fees, gas, travel hours, etc. for your overhead)

Sub-Contractors:

I) Bids
1) Labor Only.
2) Material and Labor.
3) Bides include all taxes.
4) Only from Licensed, Bonded and Insured for work performed.

II) Sub-Contractors for Duration of Project
1) General Liability Insurance.
2) Bond for Performance and Completion.
3) Certificate of Workman's Compensation Insurance.
4) References.

Material Supplier Considerations:

1) Local, Out-of-Town, Internet or Direct Buy
2) Complete Package
3) Included in Sub-Contractor's Bid
4) 'By Line' Item
5) Specialties
6) Material and Supplier's Quantity

Additional Items to Consider:

1) Total Package Bids – many items that company has in stock.
2) Variable Degrees of Fulfillment – 100%, 96%, 93% (adjusted load)
3) Alternative Bids – i.e. bids on different items (add/subtract from other bids)
4) Line Items – i.e. split two or more from different companies.
5) Quote Valid for 10, 30, 60, or 90 days?

6) Price Lock – goes with #5 above.
7) Advanced Payment Discount?
8) Pre-Payment Storage – how long will company hold materials their yard. This saves money on storage and protects your materials from damage (wind, water, theft, etc.
9) No Large Deliveries prior to Weekends – you should have a fenced area or secure storage for material and equipment. If you are not staying on site, you may want to consider a guard, additional police patrols, guard animals, security lights and/or security system.

Paperwork, Insurance & Other Services

Now that you have your land, house plans and building costs, you need to assemble some required paperwork. This will also include insurance; an attorney to go over the paperwork; and a bookkeeper to track the accounting and payroll.

I. Building Plans need to be approved by building department
II. Building Permit is required – aggregate square footage
III. Insurance Estimates for:
　1) General Liability
　2) Builders Risk
　3) Completion Bond
　4) Workman's Compensation
　5) Homeowner's Insurance (once completed)
　6) Flood Insurance (if applicable)
　7) Home Owner's Warranty
IV. Attorney
V. Appraisal from Bank or Private Firm for Pre- and Post-Construction. Check with company about a discount for doing both.
VI. Survey Estimate for Required Surveys. Check with company about discount for doing both Pre- and Post-Construction Survey.
VII. Accounting & Payroll Paperwork – recommend hiring professional.
　1) Construction Account
　2) Escrow Account
　3) Joint Checking Agreement
　4) Material Invoices and Taxes
　5) Labor Invoices and Taxes.
　6) 10% Retention on Sub-Contractors and Lien Releases
　7) 1099 Tax Form (if needed)
VIII. Title Company

CHAPTER 3
Ready, Set, Build

FINANCING

Now that you have all your paperwork together, you need to decide how you want to do the financing for your dream home. Here are some options:

1) Local or Out-of-State.
2) VA, FHA, Conventional, etc.
3) Network – three or more financial institutions.
4) Construction and Permanent – roll-over.
5) Terms, Originations, Loan Fees, Length and Percentage Rate.

Get Pre-Approval/Approval for:

1) Interim Construction Loan
2) Letter of Financial Responsibility (building dept.), if applicable.
3) Permanent Home Financing.

You should contact at least three different banks with the plans and paperwork to make the best deal possible. Find out if there are discounts for:

1) Using a Bank-Approved Appraiser.
2) Request a discount, or to drop origination fees, if both construction and permanent financing are obtained from the same bank.
3) Ask about low interest loans with long payout (30-35 years) that have no pre-payment penalties. Double up on your mortgage payments. Even an additional $50.00 per month applied to the principle of the mortgage will reduce the interest over the life of the loan.

SCHEDULING and CONSTRUCTION

Once you have acquired your interim construction loan, you are ready to get started and it's time to get everyone on board. You will need to:

1) Get Property Appraised – lender will require.
2) Get Required Insurances – lender will require.
3) Get Building Permits.
4) Get Construction Account and Accountant.

5) Contact Sub-Contractors for Scheduling.
6) Contact Materials Supplier with 10-day Start-up Time.
7) Prepare Project Schedule that includes:
   a) Work Performance.
   b) Material Orders.
   c) Delivery Schedules.
   d) Call Backs (to sub-contractors for finish work).
   e) Inspections.
   f) Progress Payments.

Additional Thoughts

It is best to set hours for construction. If you are going to be doing the work yourself, this is even more important. You need to set hours so that you can complete your building project on time. However, always keep in mind that this is not always possible, so plan for cost overruns and delays.

If you plan a project that may be objectionable to the surrounding community, residents may slow, alter or stop your progress of your project altogether. This could be very costly to you or your business, even if approved with existing zoning laws.

A myriad of things can or may go awry. So plan for this and keep positive. Try to keep on schedule as close as possible.

Always SECURE, PROTECT & GUARD all materials and the construction site all the time. This is especially true at night, on weekends, holidays and during adverse weather conditions. Ensure all materials have been braced and weighed down.

For insurance purposes, it is better to fence off the site, if possible. Always follow all safety guidelines and have disclosures to protect you, the bank and the insurance company.

I have included some additional checklists you may want to use for items I have not covered above. PLEASE REMEMBER... these are guidelines only. Always check with your local building department and/or planning and zoning office for specific codes for your area.

CHAPTER 4

Building Advisory Group (BAG) Services

LEVEL 1 - Inspections & Consultation

As the owner of this guide, I am committed to assisting you through the completion of your dream house and understand that some wish to have professional advice throughout the project. As such, I have developed two levels of personal service for your construction.

The first level, "Inspections & Consultation," includes four progress inspections that will ensure your house is being built according to specifications. It also includes 48 hours of consultation.

These services have no hidden fees and include all costs for material, labor, subcontractors and taxes through the completion of your home construction project. The following inspections include the primary building only.

Inspection #1 – Building Pad Foundation:

1) Check for Correct Elevation.
2) Check Placement on Property – side, front & rear setbacks
3) Check for Square, Batter Boards, Building Line Height, Location Accuracy, Proper Angles and Abutments, Offset Protrusions and Bump-Outs.
4) Note: Compaction Test is Foundation Sub-Contractor Responsibility.

Inspection #2 – Building Pad prior to Concrete Pour:

1) Check for Correct Elevation.
2) Check all Setbacks – front, side & rear.
3) Check Square, Angles, Offset, Protrusions, Abutments, Bump-outs, Height Variations and Straightness.
4) Check Shutoffs, Control Joints and Expansion Joints.
5) Check Footing and Depth
6) Check Slab Thickness, Rebar Placement, Plumbing Locations, HVAC Insets or Ducts, Radiant Heat, Electrical Insets and any other Special Insets as needed according to plans and specifications before concrete is poured.

Inspection #3 – Wall Framing Accuracy (prior to Fireplace Framing):

1) Check Dimensions, Electrical, Plumbing & HVAC Openings.
2) Check Door & Window Placements.
3) Check Soffit and Soffit Vents, as well as Facia Gable End Vents.

Inspection #4 – Brick Molding (after all walls, ceilings, roof, garage, porch, etc. and prior to Insulation and Sheetrock):

1) Check Plumbing, HVAC & Electrical Recesses.
2) Check Arches, Exterior, Ceiling Heights & Slopes
3) Check for Special Allowances like Irons, Board Niches, Plant Shelves, etc.

CONSULTATION:

48 man-hours are provided to assist you with resolving any reported problems or issues that may arise. All questions and issues will be answered to the best of my agent's abilities. All final decisions are to be performed by you, the owner/general contractor.

Any changes, deviations, re-inspections, rework or incident by the owner/general contractor, or their sub-contractors or agents, will increase job costs, thereby increasing the final project cost of the project based on any contract with the Building Advisory Group.

LEVEL 2 – Construction Coordinator with Inspections & Consultation

Level 2 will include all services offered in Level 1 above and will include a Construction Coordinator that will assist the owner/general contractor as an advocate to bridge any gaps between the sub-contractors. Along with the four inspections and 48 man-hours of consultation, we will provide:

I) Project Scheduling of all Sub-Contractors and Crews.
II) Daily Logs
    1) Log #1:
        a) Manpower of Sub-Contractor Reports.
        b) Number of Workers on Site.
        c) Skilled and Unskilled Labor Force.
        d) Tradesmen Required.
        e) Equipment & Materials on Site.
        f) Type of Work Performed.
    2) Log #2: Job Quality, Discrepancies or Time Delay Reports
    3) Log #3: Time Cards as needed.

4) Log #4: Progress Reports for owner, accountant and bank for repayment.
5) Log #5: Material Tracking and Draws from Suppliers and Sub-Contractors.

NOTES: Any and all field or lab inspections required by plans or specifications are to be completed by owner/general contractor agents. Some of these include, but are not limited to, compaction tests, concrete mix design and/or slump test, compression test, geological technical test and environmental test.

Any deviations, change orders, math discrepancies, or pricing problems will be reported to the owner/general contractor who will make all final decisions.

Any dispute of the final total price of building project shall be audited by an independent CPA for accuracy and be paid for by the owner/general contractor with audit honored by both parties.

Contract between owner/agent, owner/agent-representative/agent.

Appendix
- Checklists
- Notes
- Order Form

Minimum Recommended Square Footage

The following is a rough rule of thumb. Please check your local building codes for specifics.

Room	Square Feet
Living Room	221
Family Room	221
Den	221
Study/Media/Library	180
Kitchen	130
Dining Room	130
Nook	110
Master with Closet	204
Other Bedroom with Closet	168
Bath	56
Laundry	48
Hall	64
Linen Closet	12
Guest Closet	12
HVAC	42
Water Heater	12
Single-Car Garage	264

Desired Rooms Checklist

Bedrooms

- One Bedroom_____
- Two Bedroom_____
- Three Bedroom_____
- Four Bedroom_____
- Other_____

- o Office_____
- **TOTAL:_____**

Bathrooms

- One_____
- 1-1/2_____
- 1-3/4_____
- Two_____
- 2-1/2_____
- 2-3/4_____
- Threee_____
- Other_____

TOTAL:_____

Kitchen/Nook/Dining

- Kitchen_____
- Country Kitchen_____
- Nook_____
- Dining_____
- Other_____

TOTAL:____

Living Areas

- o Living Room_____
- o Den_____
- o Family Room_____
- o Media Room_____
- o Study_____
- o Library_____

o Other_____

- o Library_____
- o Office_____

TOTAL:____

Garage

- o 1 Car_____
- o 2 Cars_____
- o 3 Cars_____
- o Attached_____
- o Detached_____
- o Other_____

TOTAL:____

Outcrop Buildings

- o Barn_____
- o Workshop_____
- o Shed_____
- o Well House_____
- o Other_____

TOTAL:____

Total Desires Square Feet:_____

_____

House Style Checklist

Total Square Footage

- 1,000 – 1,500
- 1,500 – 2,000
- 2,000 – 2,500
- 2,500 - 3,000
- 3,000+

Home Style

- Ranch
- Contemporary
- Tudor
- French Provincial
- Victorian
- Traditional
- Southwest
- Spanish
- Other

Home Elevation

- One Story
- 1-1/2 Story
- Two Story
- Split Level
- Multi-Level
- Basement

Roof Type

- Shed/Lean to
- Gable
- Hip
- Gable/Hip Combo
- Flat
- Dutch Gable
- Mansurd
- Gambrel
- Other

Exterior Finish

- Wood
- Vinyl
- Metal
- Stucco
- Brick
- Stone
- comb
- Other

Roof Finish

- Shingle/Shake
- Composition
- Tile
- Metal
- Rubber
- Other

Sweat Equity Checklist

- Install Insulation*
- Haul Off Debris
- Painting*
- Hand Grading
- Build Wood Fence
- Sprinkler System
- Landscape
- Final Cleaning
- Tile Grouting*
- Lay Floor Tile*
- Lay Wood Floor*
- Tile Bathroom
- Other_____

CAUTION: The items must be done with no time delay of schedule.

- Items marked must be completed for the final inspection

Tax Checklist

- Property Tax
- Parks and Recreation Tax Assessment
- School Tax
- Road Tax
- Sewer, Water & Garbage Tax
- Energy Tax (CO_2) Surcharge
- Bonds, Special Bond Assessment
- Boat/Motorhome
- Domestic Animal Tax (Pets)
- Special Usage Tax
- Community Assessment/Fees
- Other

Additional Considerations Checklist

Y	N	
O	O	Flood Zone – Mud Slides – Erosion Area
O	O	Private/Public Water Source – Well – Cistern
O	O	Water Quality and Source – shallow or artesian
O	O	Parks & Recreation – Migration/Wetlands – Wildlfe
O	O	City/County Ordinance or Agreements
O	O	City/County Planning & Zoning
O	O	City/County/State Engineering and Roads Department
O	O	Easements – Right of Ways – Encroachments and Accesses
O	O	Landfills – Contaminates – Air, Water & Soil
O	O	Insects – Pests – Molds – Vegetation – Fungus
O	O	Pollution – Natural/Man-made
O	O	Noise – Traffic - Chemical Odors – Lights
O	O	Police – Fire – Medical
O	O	Handicap – Special Events Facility
O	O	Views – Pools, Towers, Recreation Areas, Church & Schools.
O	O	Landscape – Minimum band or prohibited Plants – Grades
O	O	Deforestation – Reshape Topography – Drainage – Retaining Walls
O	O	Causeways – Diverters – Culverts
O	O	Public Utilities – water/sewage/garbage/electric/telephone/cable/gas
O	O	Septic Tank – Leach lines and field/peak test
O	O	Well Water Metered – acre feet
O	O	Earthquake – Hurricane – Tornado – Tide Surges

Building Advisory Group

Initial Consultation = $50.00

Materials Take-off Estimate = Depends on Square Footage

Level 1 Services = Job Cost x .0395%

Level 2 Services = Job Cost x .0795%

Contact:
Dave Roork
Roswell, New Mexico
(575) 626-5837